PRE CHRISTIAN WINTERS

Yule

The winter of our ancestors was a world of limited light. So, Yule became a fire festival. Anglo-Saxon Iul was a word that means "wheel" and the spokes represent the festivals and old equinoxes.

According to the Germanic calendar, there were six tides of sixty-days in a year. Yuletide was celebrated in December and January.

Juleiss, the Nordic Yule, lasted until Twelfth night. During this period, there was no baking or coffee brewing and women weren't allowed to spin.

Yule was the shortest day of the year. The Winter Solstice was also the shortest day. It was a time when the veil between physical and spiritual worlds was thinnest. Ancestors could visit their loved ones and return to the physical world.

To help them get home, one candle was lit in certain areas.

Yule was the season of the Sun God's rebirth, which brought light and warmth back to the world and extended days. On hillstops, communal fires were lit and homes were decorated with evergreens. Pliny, the Elder of Britain said that Druids would gather mistletoe during this season and sacrifice a white Bull.

Holly King

Celtic legends tell of the battle between the Holly King (or Oak King) twins, who are both two aspects of one God. Each twin governs half a year, fighting for the Goddess' hand and the control of the seasons. The Summer Solstice is when the Oak King rules. Depicted as the Green Man in the illustration, the Holly King comes back and fights the Oak King. He does not succumb to his defeat and retreats to Caer Arianrhod. This is the castle of the ever-turning silver wheel. He must learn from Arianrhod the Goddess of Reincarnation before he is reborn at the Winter Solstice.

The Holly King is now the king of the seasons, having won the Summer Solstice. The days grow shorter and cooler during the summer heat. Mid-winter is the best time to be outside.

Oak Kings is back and fights again with the Holly King. This ends his reign and returns the world to longer, warmer days.

Father Christmas

His roots are likely to be with the Holly King, who is often depicted as wearing a long green hooded coat and a wreath or mistletoe of holly or holly.

Odin was Jul in midwinter. He wore a blue cloak and gave gifts to the good, while punishing the poor.

St Nicholas was brought by the Normans to Britain by Richard Smart, the Rector of Plymtree in the 15th century. He is referred to as Lord Christmas by Smart around 1435. However, he isn't the one bringing gifts to children; he is more of a figurehead for adult celebrations. This tradition continued until Puritan times, when Christmas was being curbed.

Even though he was referred to as an old gentleman who enjoyed the celebrations without excessive, those who supported Christmas referred to him more as Old Christmas. He was often seen in mommers plays, and in 1822 Clement C Moore created the image of Father Christmas we now know in his poem, 'The Night Before Christmas.' This was American. In Britain, Father Christmas wore a holly crown while drinking from a tankard in the 1840s.

He was the child's gift-giver by the 1870s, merging with Santa Claus and St Nicholas. His outfits were varied though. He can be seen wearing red, green brown, and red on Victorian cards.

Coca Cola's 1931 advertisement established the Father Christmas figure we know today.

Yule Log

It is now a popular cake, but it was originally a log that was used to heat the hearth. Its origins are believed to be in Germanic Paganism and the Winter Solstice. It is a European tradition.

It was believed that the sun would remain stationary for 12 days during

December. Therefore, it was important to keep the Yule Log lit so that the sun will move again.

Robert Herrick is the first to mention the Yule Log. He was a clergyman from the 1620/30s. He described the log as being brought by a group males, who were then rewarded with beer. He noted that the fire to light the log was always started with a remnant from the previous year. The log's remnant was kept in order to bring about prosperity the next year.

Yule, which is Norse for "wheel", also means Yule in Norse. The Norse believed that the sun was a wheel made of fire that moved from the Earth to the Sun. Their traditions date back thousands of years before Christianity. To ask for protection, their Yule Logs were decorated with evergreens and yew, Holly, Fir, and Runes.

Julesvenn

He is a Norse mythological figure. He is a figure that looks a lot like Santa Claus, except that he is wearing blue or white. He calls Christmas Eve to bring presents to children. He does not climb down the chimney, but he knocks at the front door. Lucky barley stalks are also left around his house by him.

Yule Goat

It is the oldest figure in the Scandinavian Yule collection.

A practice similar to the Welsh Mari Llwyd or the Wassail was common in the past. The practice of dressing up in costumes was common among young people. They would travel from one door to the next singing and performing small plays. They were accompanied on their journey by the Yule Goat, who gave them food and other gifts.

The Yule Goat can be seen today mostly as an ornament, made of straw and decorated using ribbons. Some towns even have their own Yule Goats

Display the Gavle Goat, for instance, in Sweden. It stands at 13m high and has been displayed each year since 1966. Although it is supposed to remain upright for the entire Yuletide season, it often burns down before that happens. The 1977 goat only lasted six hours. Follow the Gavlebocken on Twitter to keep up-to-date about his status.

Odin

Odin, the father of all gods, is a Nordic and Northern German deity. He was a warrior god who led a great hunt at Yule. Many believe he traveled to Earth disguised at this time to check on the happiness of communities. He was pictured wearing a long, blue-colored hooded cloak. He traveled the skies with his eight-legged horse Sleipnir to bring bread to those who were in need.

Traditions grew over time and children began to leave their boots behind with all kinds of goodies in them. Sleipnir is straw, carrots, and sugar. They would place their boots near the fire, and Odin would reward them by giving them gifts and treats.

Joulupukki

He is the principal Christmas figure of Finland. This Scandinavian character is closely connected to Woden in Germanic mythology. Although he was originally a Yule goat, he has become a Santa-like figure. He wears a warm red fur-trimmed jacket and matching trousers. He lives in Lapland with his wife and has a workshop up in the mountains of Korvatunturi. Tontu are his helpers, but they aren't elves. They are small humans who dress in the same way as him. Joulupukki is able to pull a reindeer-powered sleigh, but it won't fly.

As he knocks on front doors to inquire if any children are inside, he has a walking stick.

Mari Llwyd

Mari Llwyd (or Grey Mare) is a horse figure who accompanies singing groups. This custom is similar to the Yule Goat in Wales. Singing groups would go door-to-door singing in an attempt to gain entry. One side could conduct a pwnco (or contest) through the other at the front door. The group won and was allowed to go inside, where they could receive food, gifts, or even money. The Mari would run wild around the house, snapping its jaws, and creating chaos before they left for the next house.

Horses were a person covered in long clothes that covered his head and feet. He would use the clacking jaws to operate the horse skull made of wood, cloth, or cardboard. Other characters were sometimes included in the group, such as Punch and Judy.

Mari Llwyd's origins could have been pre-christian. Romans had Epona, a goddess of horses. Rhiannon, a Welsh goddess, is also associated with riding white horses.

The Mari Llwyd was criticized by chapels, who called it barbaric, pagan, and promoted drunken rowdy behavior. It was almost extinct by the 1960's, but it is slowly being revived.

Faeries

Believers in faeries are older than angel beliefs. Their roots are mythology and they were mysterious mischievous and frightening beings similar to humans who lived in great forests across Europe. They protected children from evil. Ellyllon is the Welsh name for the Faeries of the Valleys and Groves. Their three passions in life include silk, toadstools, and human children. They are small creatures that love children and do not mean any harm. Others faeries may also live in hollybushes, which could explain their inclusion in Christmas festivities. It is said that the Midwinter story involves Midwinter and the faeries.

The faeries once lived in Europe's great forests. They were kind-hearted and generous and were given magic powers by the Gods, Goddesses and Gods. They were very fond of children, and the Faery Queen would invite everyone into the forest at Midwinter. The Faery Queen was introduced to each child and they could ask for one gift. After kissing each child on the cheek, the Queen led them to the edge of the forest, where they waited for their parents. They had to keep their wishes secret or they wouldn't be fulfilled.

Faeries evolved eventually from tiny creatures to being able to fly and use wands. When we place a faery above the Christmas tree, it symbolizes the forest and the Yule for the faeries.

Mistletoe

Mistletoe is a sacred European plant. It attaches to trees to absorb nutrients. Two white bulls were sacrificed by the Druids to the Mistletoe of the sacred Oak while prayers were being said.

This Mistletoe will make you prosperous. It protected against goblins and lightning strikes.

Also, mistletoe was associated with the Roman Saturnalia festival. In Scandinavia, it was also a symbol for peace. It was required to declare a truce for enemies below. It was used to keep away evil spirits and witches in the home during the Middle Ages.

A mistletoe-filled kissing ball became very popular in the 18th century, when most people didn't believe in witches. The kissing ball was so attractive that any lady who stood under it could not resist being kissed. It didn't always signify romance, but it could also be a kiss that will last a lifetime.

Mistletoe is a mythological character in Norse mythology.

Frigga, a goddess of love, was once a reality. Balder, the God of Summer Sun, was her son. Balder had nightmares of death, so Frigga was worried about him. Frigga knew that the world would end if Balder died. Frigga asked the elements Fire, Earth, Water, Earth, and Water to promise not to harm Balder.

Balder was however aided by Loki, an enemy who knew the name of a plant Frigga had forgotten, Mistletoe. Loki took some Mistletoe and made an arrow head. He gave it to Hoder the blind God of Winter, who shot Balder.

Balder died, and all Gods were saddened. Odin sent his son Hermod, to Hel, Goddess of Death, to plead for his release. Hel accepted, provided that all living things on Earth wept. Everything did except Loki. Balder was forced to stay in the Underworld until Ragnarok when the world was destroyed. He could then return.

Frigga made Mistletoe her sacred plant. It is believed that her tears for Balder turned into white berries. She decreed that no one should be hurt by it.

Yule Boar

Sow Day is an ancient tradition in Northern Europe, when a boar is killed on 17 December for Yule feast. This is a reminder of when the

Freya, the Norse goddess of fertility Freya was afraid to kill boar. It was sacrificed at the darkest hour of the year to encourage the return of sunlight.

According to Scandinavian myths Freya had a magical golden boar called Gullinbursti, or Golden Bristles. It was named so because it could run as fast and with the same speed as horses, and glowed with a glowing golden light. Its sacrifice was likely to symbolize the end of the old sun and the birth of the new.

Yule Boars were also used to swear oaths. Yule was the time when the best boars from the herd were brought into a hall. Freya would be the first to hear and make oaths to anyone who made them. After all oaths had been sworn, the boar was killed and eaten.

Mother's Night

Mothers Night was a celebration of motherhood in 725 by Historian Bede. He described it in his book "De temporum Ratio" as:

"The year began on the 8th of January, when we celebrate The Birth of the Lord. This night is sacred to us and was called Mothers Night by the heathen Modranecht because of all the rituals they performed that night.

Mothers Night was first observed in the Germanic regions, Gaul, Italy and Spain. Its roots lie in the belief of the mother goddess and the votive stones and altars that were set up to worship them. Holda, an old Germanic Winter goddess was honored by the system. This was the night that the year was born. Mothers who were in spirit were honored and asked for protection and healing. Their grandmother or mother would make sure that all children were asleep and would then commit them to the protection a goddess, an ancestor, or one of the female ancestral deities called Disir. It was originally celebrated on Christmas Eve in Anglo Saxon times, but it is now the eve the Winter Solstice. Pagans still practice rituals for Mothers Night.

Saturnalia

Ancient Rome celebrated a winter festival. In the beginning, Saturnalia was a one-day festival on the 17th of Dec. But it soon grew to a week. It included Opalia on December 19th and Sigillaria the following day. On the 25th of December was "Dies natalis Solis Invicti", the birthday celebration for Sol, or the Sun God, and it was celebrated. Augustus, Emperor of Rome, tried to decrease

Saturnalia up to three days, Caligula up to five.

Saturnalia was an occasion to honor the Roman god Saturn, who is the god of sowing and seed. The statue of Saturn was kept in the temple for the majority of the year. However, at Saturnalia, his feet were untied to show his freedom.

Saturnalia was described by Catullus, the poet, as "the best of times". In the hope of a good harvest next year, banquets and sacrifices were made at the temples. It was a time for celebration and a time to see family and friends. Gift exchanges were called Sigillaria. Candles and figurines were particularly popular.

Work was prohibited, all businesses were closed, and people wore brightly colored clothes instead of their everyday togas. Singing, drinking, and partying were the order of day. Even slaves were permitted to join the fun.

Role reversal occurred, slaves could become masters for the duration Saturnalia and had their food served to them. The holiday was presided over by a lord of misrule, who also gave the greeting 'Io (Yo!). Saturnalia.

Candles

The winter festivals were centered on light, which was and is still a central theme. Saturnalia was the time when the gift of light came in the form a candle. Before that, bonfires were lit in order to promote the Sun's return. The Christmas tradition of light carried on as a bonfire. A large candle was lit to commemorate the birth of Christ in the early days of Christianity. This tradition continued throughout the year. Placed in wreaths, or in windows, candles were used. For the Plygain tradition in Wales, whole churches were lit by candlelight. In Sweden, St Lucia is commemorated by the crown and small lit tapers.

Gift giving

Sigillaria, which was celebrated on the 23rd December, was a day for exchanging gifts within the Roman Empire. The type of gift you received and gave was determined by your financial situation. You could give simple gifts like toothpicks, candles or books. Or, you could gift a slave if your budget allows. While bosses might give toys to children, they would also give toys to them.

Gifts to clients Gifts can also be associated with the birth and life of Jesus, as well as the wise men who traveled to the stable to give their gifts of gold and frankincense to myrrh.

Wreaths

The origins of the wreath can be traced back to Roman times. As a symbol for victory, wreaths were put on the heads of Olympic athletes. The wreath represented hope for the Germanic pagans, a sign of Spring's return and renewed light and warmth.

The Advent wreath was adopted by Christians in the 16th century. It consisted of a ring made of evergreens, which represented the continued life of Jesus and winter. There were four candles around the circumference and one at the center. The blood of the Crucifixion was represented by the Holly's berries.

The first candle was lit on Advent's first week. The second candle was lit on Advent's second week. And so on, until Christmas Eve, when the fifth candle was lit to commemorate the birth of Jesus.

Elves

European paganism is the origin of the elf. They were small creatures that lived underground, in springs, wells, forests and the ground. It was believed that the elf protected the house from evil in Scandinavia. If you treat the elf well, it will be kind to you. However, if you treat it poorly, it will play tricks on you and cause nightmares. It was in the best interest of the household that the elf be treated well, and not rude.

Santa Claus was described in 1823 as a "right jolly old Elf" in A Visit From St Nicholas. Louisa May Alcott published a book on Christmas elves in 1850, but it was never published. In the middle 1800s, Scandinavian writers also revealed the true purpose for Christmas elves. It was to care for the reindeer and sleigh

as well as keep the nice and naughty lists up-to-date. You would receive coal if
you were unruly.

Godey's Lady Book 1873 showed Santa with toys and elves. They are shown
here today, posing with Santa at North Pole. They are often seen in green and
red, with pointed hats.

Tomte

The Winter Solstice is a Scandinavian gift-giver. He stands about three feet
tall, has a long white hair and wears colorful clothes. The Tomte was thought
to have been the soul of the first person to live in the house in ancient times.
Porridge was left for the Tomte as a reminder of ancestor worship. The Tomte
protects his home as long as he receives good treatment.

MEDIEVAL CHRISTMAS

Carols

It's difficult to pinpoint when the first people began singing. Songs and dances
may have been around as long as people, and it is possible that our pagan
ancestors sang or danced during their winter festivals.

The first hymns appeared in the years following Jesus's death. There was the
Angel's Hymn of AD 129 and the Comas of Jerusalem hymn for Christmas.
Most hymns at that time were in Latin, which was difficult for most people to
understand. This was changed when St Francis started his Nativities in 1223.
These were songs that told the story and were called canticles. They were
sometimes produced in the language the audience understood and enjoyed to
help them understand what they were hearing and seeing. A 1410 song
describes Mary and Joseph as they travel through Bethlehem, meeting various
people along the route.

French word "Carol" originally meant a song that could easily be danced to.
Carols could be written for each of the four seasons. They were banned in
churches by Tudor times as they were too literal and prohibited from being

sang in the home. They might also be sung in the home by traveling groups, who may alter the lyrics to suit their audience. They might be sung by people going about their daily work to pass the time.

Wynken de Worde, a London printer and publisher, wrote the Boars Head Carol in 1521. It was included in his Christmasse Carolles. It tells the tale of the boar's head arriving at the dinner table.

The singing of Christmas carols was stopped when the Puritans took power in Britain. Although people did continue singing in secret, the songs remained largely unheard in public until William Sandys and Davis Gilbert started to travel around villages collecting them in Victorian times. Sandy's Christmas Carols Collection from the 15th century to the end the 17th century was published by Davis Gilbert in 1833. Gilbert published his collections 1822-1823.

Carol singing was a big hit in Victorian times. They were popularized by singing them in the streets and choirs formed to sing them at Christmas services.

In 1918, Nine lessons from Kings College Cambridge were first broadcast to commemorate the end of the First World War.

Calendar of 354 AD

This year, a calendar was created for Valentinus, a Roman Christian. It is the first reference to a 25th December feast date. It also records astrological phenomena and imperial anniversaries. Although pagan celebrations were prohibited, some festivals were still observed. Saturnalia and Dies Natalis Sol Invictus, which is the Roman Sun God of Roman Empire on 25 December, are both recorded. It also mentions '25 Dec

....natus Christus Betleem Judeae' December 25th Christ born in Bethlehem.

This calendar indicates that Christians and Pagans co-existed at the time, even though some pagan celebrations, such as games, gift giving, and races, were being banned.

Shepherds

The Gospel of Luke describes shepherds. They tend to their flocks in the fields that night of Jesus's birthday. They are tended to their flocks by an angel who informs them about the birth and places to find the baby. The angel told them to go into Bethlehem, and they found him in a stable.

It is still disputed as to when Jesus was actually born. It was the saint's death date that was more important in ancient times than Jesus' birth date. As it is unlikely that they would have been doing so in winter, some believe Jesus was born in Spring. It is notable, too, that the angel could have appeared before many other notable and important people on Earth but chose to appear to the humble shepherd.

The Wise Men

Matthew Chapter 1 verses 1 to 3 is the most well-known version of the wise men.

"After Jesus was born at Bethlehem in Judea during the time King

Herod, Magi of the East, came to Jerusalem to ask, "Where is the one who was born King of the Jews?" We saw his star in east and came to worship him.

Matthew's account does not list the names or number of Magi. Perhaps we have come to believe that there were three Magi, as three gifts were presented to Jesus. Although the Magi are astrologers, wise men can sometimes be called kings.

It is not clear when the Magi visited. Matthew simply says that it took place 'after Jesus was born. They followed his star, but they were already far from their stable when they arrived. Matthew Chapter 2 verse 11 reveals this.

"They came to the house and saw the child and his mother Mary. They bowed down before him and worshipped him. They opened their treasures to give him gifts of gold, incense, and myrrh.

A sixth-century mosaic from the basilica Sant Apollinaire, Italy shows an early image of the Magi. This image shows them carrying gifts against a background of palm trees.

The Star of Bethlehem

Only in Matthew's Nativity do the wise men follow the star that shows the birthplace of Jesus.

The star is an emblem of hope for Christians and a sign that marks the coming of the Messiah. Astronomers have linked the star to many cosmic phenomena to try to understand what the wise men may have seen.

Some suggest that the star could have been a light from the birth of another star or a comet. Chinese astronomers found a comet in Capricorn 5 BC. In 4 BC, far-east astronomers saw a new star within the northern constellation Aquila. It is likely that the star was not a comet, as comets were believed to be bad omens. However, the wise men were astronomers. It could have been an nova, as they fade slowly and appear again.

It was, according to all the wise men who saw it, a significant event in the night sky.

Ignatius, who died in Ad 107, wrote that it was

"A star that shone in heaven above all the stars, its brightness caused excitement"

The Proto evangelium of James was authored

"Wise men say to Herod, "We saw how an indescribably large star shone."

We have taken these stars and dimmed their brightness so they don't shine anymore, and we now know that Israel had a king.

Eusebius, fourth-century church historian, concluded that after extensive research

"The star was new and unheard of among the usual lights in heaven, a star that was not like the others, unusual and strange, not one of many stars, but new and fresh"

Kepler, an astronomer, suggested that three combinations of Saturn and Jupiter in the year 7 BC might have been the star. Although it appears to have occurred in 12 BC, the appearance of Halley's Comet may also be linked to this star.
Epiphany

Epiphany is derived from the Greek Epiphaneia, which means a manifestation or appearance. This day commemorates the human manifestation of God, Jesus Christ. It is rooted in Eastern Christianity, which celebrates the visit of the Magi and Jesus. The Western Christian Church created a twelve-day festival by separating the nativity from the 25th December, sometime before 354

In the history of Christianity, Epiphany's date was established quite early. Ammianus Marcellinus was a Roman soldier and historian who referred to a feast on this date in 361AD. In 385 AD, Silvia, a pilgrim also known as Silvia, described an Epiphany celebration that took place in Jerusalem or Bethlehem in 385 AD.

St Gregory of Nazianzus, on 25 December 380, called the day Theophany. This was an alternative to nativity. On the 6th and the 7th of January, sermons were read to commemorate the visitation and birth of the Magi.
Hunting the Wren

The wren was sacred to the Druids. It represented wisdom and divinity, and it would have been unlucky to harm it. In the future, this philosophy was lost.

Hunting the wren was an ancient tradition. It was held on St Stephens Day (26th December). This may have been due to the legend of St Stephen being betrayed in the chattering birds. This custom was also practiced in England.

France, Ireland, and Wales. People set out early in the morning to capture the wren. The bird was then returned to its home or church, where it was killed.

There were also variations that included young men called "wren boys", who chased and beat wrens from the bushes. The bird was secured to a pole and decorated with ribbons. It was then paraded around the town. The feathers of the bird would be given away for a fee as they were considered lucky.

The bird would sometimes be kept alive, put in a cage, and paraded around the town. People would often pay for the opportunity to see a fake bird and then reward their captors with food or wassail.

King Wenceslas

He is also known as Vaclav The Good. He was the Duke of Bohemia between 907 and 935. When Wenceslas turned thirteen, his father, also the Duke de Bohemia, died. Wenceslas was forced to wait until he turned eighteen to take the throne. He waited while his mother Drahomira ruled.

Wenceslas, once a ruler, established a law system that was successful and began building churches. But his most famous memory is the story of the poor man who gathered wood for the Feast of Stephen. Wenceslas gave the food and wine to the poor man and carried it through the snowstorm to his house. Although it's not certain if this tale is true, it was the subject of a Czech poet Vaclav Adest Floridum's 1847 poem. J M Neale wrote the words to a 13th-century springtime carol, titled 'Tempus Adest Floridum', or 'It's time for Flowering', sometime after that.

Boleslav, Wenceslas' brother, was also his. He was jealous of Wenceslas and invited him to a feast with his intention of killing him. In fact, he stabbed him while he was on his way to church. Wenceslas was made the patron saint in the Czech Republic after he was martyred.

The story of Wenceslas was printed on British Christmas stamps in 1973.

Cristes Maesse
In the year 1038, the first known mention of Christmas was made in a book in Saxon England. Its meaning was Festival of Christ.

Wassail

"Waes hael" is an Anglo Saxon word that means, "be in good health." Silure Prince Vortigern was presented by Rowena, a Saxon woman. She gave him a glass of wine and toasted him with the words Waes hael. Vortigern wed Rowena, and his kingdom fell under the control of the Saxons.

To be shared around the table, the wassail bowl had to be quite large. It contained mulled ale, which was made with roasted apples, curdled milk, eggs, ginger, nutmeg, and sugar. This drink is called 'lambswool.

Wassail was a form of exchange in Middle Ages between lords or peasants. It was similar to carolling, where the lord gave food and drink in exchange for goodwill.

Wassail can become rowdy though, with drunken revellers entering homes to demand more food and drink. The householder who refuses to drink or eat might be cursed.

You could also use the Wassail to bless fruit trees, encouraging good harvests and scaring away evil spirits.

Childermass Day
Also known as Holy Innocents Day. After being ordained for the day, some European towns granted a boy charge to their town on 28 December.

Children were beaten in England to remember Herod's cruelty when he ordered all children below two years old to be executed. Edward IV refused to crown Edward IV on this day because it was considered a day of bad luck.
Christmas at Court
William the Conqueror, in 1066, chose Christmas Day as his coronation day. It was symbolic of William the Conqueror, King of the Realm, joining God the King Of Heaven. At the monarch's court, Christmas was an integral part of daily life. Christmas was a time of feasting, ceremonies and displays

Pageantry and entertainment. A lot of medieval networking would have been possible.

The audience of the monarch would have included nobles and peers. Nobody would have declined to be invited to Christmas court. It would have offended the monarch and they would have missed the chance to dress up, eat at the feast, and get gossipy. There were gifts exchanged, ties were made with other countries, titles were bestowed, and honours were given. The event concluded with dances and tournaments.

The poor, however, just watched. The poor might be able to see the nobility and royals as they travel to the feast. They might even be able to eat leftovers from the banquets if they were fortunate. The average kitchen produces twenty-four courses, and they always make a little more to feed the poor as well as themselves. The locals may offer their services to entertain the monarch and his guests in return for leftovers. They might even read poetry or act.

The monarch used Christmas Day to lay hands. He also used the healing power that Kings and Queens believed they had to heal skin conditions.

Stockings

The Christmas stocking has no documented history, other than legend. It may have its roots in Odin's story and the children who filled their boots full of hay to reward Sleipnir, the eight-legged horse, with food.

An account of St Nicholas also includes stockings.

One time, there was a widower with three children. He had lost his entire fortune and was unable provide a dowry for his three daughters. After the girls had dried their stockings over the fireplace and washed them, St Nicholas took three bags of gold from the widower's pocket. He climbed up onto the roof to throw them down the chimney, where they fell in the stockings.

Clement Moore mentions stockings also in his 1823 poem, 'A Visit From St Nick'. Thomas Nast provided illustrations for the poem and they were included in George Webster's 1886 book, 'Santa Claus and his Works.'

St Nicholas

On 6th December, St Nicholas's feast day is celebrated. Nicholas was a fourth-century Christian saint and bishop from Myra. He is believed to have been a secret gift giver who placed coins in the stockings or shoes of those who left them. Scientists were permitted to photograph and measure the contents of

Nicholas' grave in the 1950's. He was approximately five feet six inches tall, according to 2005 research. His face was rebuilt in 2008 to show a broad chin, brow and olive skin. He also had brown eyes. The remains of St Nicholas can be found here

Located in Southern Italy.

Ashen Faggot

Devon and Somerset have a long tradition that may go back to Saxon times.

It certainly shares similarities with the Yule Log.

Bundles of Ash sticks were collected, bound together with smaller green band from the hedgerows. It was put on the fire at Christmas Eve and each band broke. A toast to good health and a wish were made. Traditions say that married women can choose from a variety of bindings and the one that breaks first will be used to determine who is the first to marry the next year.

It was said that years of bad luck would ensue if the Ashen Faggot wasn't burned. The Ash sticks' ashes were removed from the fire and lit the next year's bundle.

1085

Wiliam, the Conqueror, announced at Christmas Court in Gloucester that a census would take place. It became the Domesday Book.

1126

Henry I attempted to convince his barons at Windsor Castle to accept Matilda, his daughter, as his heir. He had no son. Matilda's cousin Stephen was crowned

King in 1135, when Henry 1 had died. This led to civil war. Matilda's son Henry, Anjou, was crowned in 1153.

1133 - 189

Henry II ruled for 34 years. He spent Christmas at twenty-four different locations during that time.

1170

Although there had been tensions between King Henry II, Archbishop of Canterbury Thomas a Beckett and Thomas a Beckett over years, it was only after Beckett's Christmas sermon when the king made the statement, 'Will not one rid me from this turbulent priest? Four knights killed Beckett on 29 December.

1207 - 1272

Henry III, in 1261, ordered 160 deer to be fed at his feast. He ordered 171 pairs shoes and gifts for paupers, as well as presents from his family.

Mince Pies

It is possible that mince pie originated in the Crusades, 13th century, when Middle East recipes were acquired by Crusaders.

Original shape of the pie was rectangular. It was filled with minced meats like beef suet, minced mutton and spices such as ginger, mace and cinnamon.

They were known as Shrid pies in Tudor times. In Stuart and Georgian times, the mince pie was considered a sign of wealth.

The mince pie was forbidden during Christmas, but they were reintroduced after the restoration of the monarchy. However, the shape was changed to circular.

In the 18th century, sugar was introduced from the West Indies. It was used to sweeten the pies. The Victorian era saw the original mince pie change to one that is easily recognized today. It was made only with fruits and spices, but there were still recipes if you wanted to use meat.

1358

Edward III entertained King David of Scotland, King John of France and King John of France even though they were his prisoner. He enjoyed hosting mid-winter tournaments.

1395

York Minster was presented with the Holy Innocents Relics by Richard II.

1397

Richard II hosted a Christmas dinner for ten thousand people, and employed about two thousand.

Schnee

The Little Ice Age was a time period in North America and Europe that lasted from the 14th century to the 19th century. Between the years 1309-1814, at least twenty-three times per year, the River Thames was frozen over. The first frost fair took place on the Thames in 1608. These artworks document the swings, stalls and games played, as well as the animals and people who were present. This may have been the inspiration for the desire to have a white Christmas every year.

Henry VIII, a sleigh rider, traveled from London's centre to Greenwich in the year 1536. The Little Ice Age snow was heavier than today and remained on the ground for longer times. People could skate on frozen rivers, ponds, and rivers.

"A Frost Fair on Thames at Temple Stairs" (1684) shows people on ice as well as horses, sledges, and games. Similar scenes are shown in other paintings. The 1814 frost fair was photographed by an artist who captured snow drifts on the river.

The harsh winter of 1814 was a reality. London was enveloped in dense fog and snow fell for days. Icicles were suspended from rooftops, and water sources frozen over. Charles Dickens, the author, would have experienced these winters. He no doubt used his memories to create his works.

Although white Christmases have become less common in recent generations, people still yearn for them.

As with White Christmas, a song written by Irving Berlin in 1940. It is a nostalgic look back at snowy Christmases long gone. This song was first performed on Bing Crosby's radio show The Kraft Music Hall Christmas Day 1941.

1460

Richard Duke of York, his son and Earl of Rutland were both killed at the Battle of Wakefield by Lancastrians. Because the battle occurred around Christmas, a truce was called to ensure that the celebrations continued.

God Rest Ye Merry Gentlemen

Although the author of the carol is not known, the lyrics are believed to be Olde English and date back to the 15th century. It was published for the first time in Christmas Carols Ancient & Modern in 1833.
1484
The Christmas court of Richard III was abuzz with activity. Worries were raised by the church and the writers of the Croyland Chronicle, who felt that the riotous music and dancing they couldn't speak of was shameful.

Boy Bishop

This was a common custom in England, and possibly other parts of the world, from the thirteenth-century onwards.

Perhaps a boy from the choristers would be chosen to parody the real bishop, from St Nicholas Day (6/12/12) until Holy Innocents Day (28/12/12). The boy would dress the same as the real bishop, with robes, a mitre, and friends serving as priests. They would bless the people of the town. For the duration, the real bishop would step down symbolically. The boy assumed control of the cathedral, and performed all ceremonies except for mass.

The custom was ended in 1542, when Henry Viii created the Church of England. It was briefly revived from 1552 to 1562.

Elizabeth I finally ended the practice.

Modern times have seen revivals, such as in Hereford in 1973 when a special service for children was held.

Plygain

This early morning service is probably pre-reformation in Wales. Plygain's time was between dawn and eight on Christmas morning, with High Mass at nine or ten. People would often stay up late or wake up early to go to their parish church. The original service was for men only, but it became open to women later. Even though Carols were forbidden by the Puritans, they would still be sung.

Clwyd, Mrs Thrale of Duffryn wrote a journal in 1774 that describes dancing and singing to the harp up until Plygain. The women spent their time decorating the house and making toffee, while the men played outside under torchlight.

People attended the service with candles because there was no lighting in the church. After prayers and a sermon, several groups of carollers took charge, with no more than one carol being sung.

Special Plygain candles began to be made in the middle 1800s. It was easy to forget that so many candles illuminated the congregation and church, it was not surprising that accidents could occur. In 1770, one parish's Plygain was halted after a man set ablaze another parishioner's head. The 'indecent behavior' of those attending the service at St Thomas's Church in Neath resulted in the ban on the service at St Thomas's Church.

In Wales, the Plygain tradition continues to be carried on.

Mumming

Mummers were groups that performed plays, dances, or music to celebrate Christmas. It started as miming. It began as miming. However, in Middle English, "Mum" means silent. Later on, words were added to the performances. These stories evolved over time.

Mummers celebrated the end of the Old Year and the rebirth of the Spring. The theme of the Holly and Oak Kings was a common one that ran through all the plays. A tale told in verse about a fight between two people.

heroes. One of them would die, but would be revived by a doctor.

Costumes played a significant role in the 16th and 17th century, especially at Court, where elaborate costumes and masques were common.

Plough Monday

It is a common celebration in agricultural communities. It was first mentioned in the 15th century as the first Monday after Twelfth night and marked the return to work. Plough gangs were groups of young men who would go around the community knocking on doors, hoping to get money or drinks. They would bring a decorated plough with them. Failure to acknowledge the gang would lead to lawns being mowed.

Plough Monday was also associated with mumming. Blackened faces were common in plays. Characters such as the fool, who wore skins with a pigs bladder and carried it on a stick, are examples of blackened faces. The 'Bessy' was an old woman and a musician. The theme of the dance was death and resurrection.

Plough Monday celebrations fell with the Industrial revolution in 19th century, but have been revived in 20th century.

Nativity

St Francis of Assisii visited Grecio in 1223. He found the chapel too small to hold midnight mass there, so he decided to build an altar in a niche on a rock nearby the square.

St Bonaventure, who died in 1274, related the story of this first living Nativity that told the Christmas story.

"Then he made a manger and brought hay, an ox, and an ass to their place. The brethren were called, and the people ran together. The forest resounded with their voices, and that glorious night was made magnificent by many bright lights and psalms.

From the 1300s, terracotta nativity sets began to appear in churches. By the

1500s they were common in wealthy homes. Materials changed and sets were made of wax or wood.

The nativity story is actually a combination of both Matthew and Luke's accounts. They each have their own stories. Matthew's version has an angel appearing to Joseph to assure him about Mary's pregnancy. So they get married.

Jesus is born in Bethlehem. The wise men later see the star and inform Herod, before Jesus bestows their gifts. Joseph receives a warning from Herod in a dream. He flees Bethlehem and heads to Egypt to escape Herod's massacre of children under two years old. Around 4 BC, Joseph is told by Herod in a dream that he has to go to Nazareth in order for him not return to Bethlehem.

According to Luke, the nativity sees Mary and Joseph traveling from Nazareth to Bethlehem to meet Jesus. They attempt to find a room in an inn, but the inn is full so Mary puts her baby in a stable. The angels visit shepherds to inform them about the birth and invite them to visit the family. Simeon, Anna and Anna praise Jesus as he is later taken to the temple. Mary and Joseph later return home to Nazareth.

One reason the accounts are different could be because the authors were writing for different audiences. Matthew was written for Jews to confirm prophecies in the Old Testament, Luke for gentile Christians to strengthen their faith. They both agree on certain points. Mary, Joseph, and Luke were together before Jesus was born. Mary was a virgin who gave birth to Jesus in Bethlehem, but they lived in Nazareth.
Snowmen

It is difficult to know when the first figures were made from snow. It could be as old or as recent as cave paintings and figurines from thousands of years ago. Bob Eckstein, a snowman researcher, suggests that an illustration from a 1380 manuscript called the Book of Hours depicts a snowman.

However, snowmen can be traced back to Victorian times. For example, Wilhelm Meyerheim's 1853 painting Children Building a Snowman. Many different designs of snowmen were then created with the advent of postcards and greeting cards.

Advertising began to use snowmen in the 20th century. On a cigar box label, a 1919 snowman is displayed next to a fir branch smoking a cigar.

The toy market eventually saw the production of snowmen. A German snowman toy that was made in 1920. It eats snowballs.

Radio and television brought Snowman characters to life through films, cartoons, and songs. Frosty the Snowman was written by Jack Rollins, Steve Nelson, and recorded by Gene Autry. The song was released December 14, 1950.

Christmas Pudding

The Frumenty of 14th-century Europe is the likely ancestor of Christmas Pudding. This porridge was made from beef, mutton and raisins. It also included wines, spices, prunes, prunes, wine, and spices. It was thickened with eggs and breadcrumbs, dried fruits, beer, spirits, and became Plum Pudding by 1595.

In 1650, it was made a Christmas dessert. In 1664, the Puritans attempted to make Christmas a day of fasting and not feasting. However, different sources disagree on whether or not the pudding was banned.

George I liked the pudding at his Christmas table, and it developed into the pudding that we all know today. The meat was left out in Victorian times.

Christmas pudding has been a tradition. To represent Jesus and his disciples, it should contain thirteen ingredients. In honour of the wise men, everyone in the household should mix the mixture using a wooden spoon. A sixpence should also be added. The sixpence will bring good luck to the one who finds it.

Turkey

The introduction of turkey to Europe was made by European explorers who traveled to the new world between the 14th- and 15th centuries. The Native Americans had been eating turkey for years. William Strickland, a British king, introduced turkey to Britain in 1526. King Henry VIII was the first British monarch to serve turkey at Christmas. A quick glance at Charles Dickens' 'A Christmas Carol' reveals that Turkey was still the meat for the wealthy in Victorian times. The prize turkey is kept in the butchers shop until Scrooge can buy it on Christmas morning. If they had the money, most families could afford beef or goose. Turkey was a rare luxury until the 1950s, when modern farming techniques made it affordable. There are currently forty-three different breeds.

Tudor Christmas Pie

Tudor Christmas Pie was created when a pigeon was stuffed in a partridge. The partridge was placed inside a chicken, while the chicken was placed inside a chicken and the chicken inside a goose. Finally, the goose was placed inside a turkey. The whole lot was then hidden in a pie-shaped coffin and served with small meats like game birds.

Lord of Misrule

This Christmas character is lost. It dates back to Roman Saturnalia, when a Lord was appointed as the manager of the festivities. He would be known today as a party planner. The reign of the Lord would start around 31 October, and last until Candlemas on February 2. The reign was mainly for twelve days of Christmas.

The Lord of Misrule had the duty to organize plays, masques feasts and mock courts. To show his authority, he wore a paper crown to hide his inability to follow the rules.

In the 16th century, Christmas was marked by the Lord of Misrule. Henry Percy was once married to Anne Boleyn, but was forced to divorce her. He employed a Lord in Misrule to help him for 30 shillings.

The household council of Princess Mary in 1525 wrote to Cardinal Wolesley, asking if they should appoint Lord of Misrule or provide "disgysyngs and plays" for the household.

The Complaint about Christmas was a pamphlet by John Taylor, a royal satirist. It describes the death of the Lord of Misrule following a meeting with several tradesmen and servants while visiting a rural region.

"All the liberty, the harmless sports, with all the merry dances, gambols and friscals through which the toiling labourers and plowswain were wont to have their spirits and hope revived for a whole 12 months are now extinct. The mad lords at Westminster have suppressed the merry lords in misrule.

Although the Lord of Misrule didn't appear in future Christmases, we might have a small remnant of him in the Christmas crackers paper crowns.

Egg Nog

Traditionally, a drink that is made from milk, cream, sugar, and whipped egg.

The spirit is then added, such as brandy or rum.

Although its history is not clear, it may have been inspired by posset, an ancient drink that was made with hot milk. Middle English for Noggin is the word "nog", which refers to a small wooden cup. Egg Nog was a popular drink among the wealthy of Britain. It was brought to America by the English colonists in 18th century.

An incident known as the "Egg Nog Riot" occurred in 1826 when American military personnel smuggled whiskey into the country to make the drink. This led to twenty court martials.

Peacock

This is not a Christmas tradition, but it was once the centerpiece of the wealthy's Christmas table. First, the bird was skinned and then cooked before being reinserted into its skin. As with its body, the beak could be covered with gold leaf. The wire frame would hold its neck in place and the tail feathers would be displayed.

Twelfth Night

Although this ended the twelve days of Christmas, it was also the end of a medieval winter festival that had been ongoing since All Hallows Eve 31 October,

It was a night of games, food and parties. The Twelfth Night Cake was also a part of the celebration. It was baked with one dried bean, and one dried pea. One on the left and one on the right. As guests arrived in the grand houses, the ladies on the left and the men on the right were given slices of cake. The night was won by the one who found the pea, and the queen was the one who got the bean. Also included were the servants.

Although the Twelfth Night cake can be elaborately decorated with icing or ornaments, it is not possible for poor families to afford sugar. The cake contained a bean, and the person who found it was the guardian of their family for one year.

This was also the time that cakes were baked before the Reformation to celebrate Epiphany. As a refreshment, priests who visited houses would receive a slice of the cake while blessing it. Although this was prohibited as with Christmas, it was revived afterward.

It is considered unlucky not to take down decorations after the holiday season ends, which is Twelfth Night. They must be removed all year by anyone who leaves them up.

There is always controversy over when Twelfth night falls. According to the church, it falls on the night before Epiphany which is January 5. Christmas started at sunset on 24 December, so the 12th night after that was the 5th of January in medieval times. Today, the 12 days of Christmas are counted starting at midnight on the 25th December. Twelfth night is the 6th January.

Twelfth Night was celebrated in some locations on the 17th of January, as if the calendar hadn't changed since 1751.

Old Christmas Day

The calendar was based on the phases of each moon. This was incorrect and was altered by Julius Caesar's astronomers. A year would contain three hundred sixty five and a half days, and be divided into twelve periods. To commemorate the reform, the month of Quirinus was renamed to July and became the Julian calendar.

This system was however also incorrect. The calendar underestimated the year by eleven minutes, fifteen seconds. Although it doesn't seem like much, every one hundred twenty eight years the calendar was off by a day. It was ten days ahead by the 16th century.

Gregory XIII, pope, decided to make it right in 1582. He shortened the eleven minutes and fifteen second time limit and got rid the extra ten days. The Gregorian calendar was widely adopted in Catholic Europe.

Protestant Europe refused to accept the new calendar. London, however, kept the Julian calendar until the middle of 18th century and was 11 days ahead of Catholic Europe.

The Calendar Act was adopted in 1751. The 14th day after 2 September 1752 was to become the 3rd. The people did not like this and it seemed as though the Government had taken eleven days from their lives. Even riots were possible. People used to celebrate Christmas on 6th January, which was the same as the new calendar. For a long time, it was called Old Christmas Day.

Pantomime

British holiday entertainment based on fairy tales and songs, with audience participation. Women are heroes and men are the 'Dames'.

Pantomime's origins can be traced back to the theatres in Greece and Rome. These raunchy plays, which were performed at Saturnalia, were outlawed by Christians. However, they resurfaced in Italy around the 15th Century as the Commedia dell arte. Many characters were involved, many of which are still recognized today. Gingurto, Coviello and the Neapolitan were boasters. Beltrama was a simple man, Gelsomino was a dashing. Harlequin was the leading character, and Columbine was his love interest. Pulchinello, also known as Mr Punch, is the longest-surviving character. He often appears at seasides along with his wife Judy, crocodile, and baby.

Covent Garden, London was the first British pantomime. John Rich, 1692, was Lincoln Inn Fields manager between 1717 and 1761. A Harlequin sorcerer performed a Harlequinade. The magic of the Harlequins sword was used to create scenes.

Pantomimes were also performed at Drury Lane in London. David Garrick,(1717

Thespian and theatre manager transformed harlequin from a silent character into a talking actor. He could point to different colours on his costumes, such as yellow for jealousy, red to love, and black to indicate that he was invisibility.

Pantomimes could sometimes be performed after a play, such as the one reviewed by The Cambrian Newspaper. It was performed in Swansea on July 18, 1806.

"A pleasant little pantomime was performed after the play with great credit. Mr Dunn was very funny in the Clown. Masterman fell quite a bit in Harlequin, but managed to make two good leaps. Mrs Potter's Columbine was a highly commendable performance that brought universal joy. Three cheers were raised by a large crowd of Gods when the last scene of the pantomime, in which was shown an admirably executed transparency of the lamented Nelson, brought forth the final scene.

This review was completed in September 1819.

Mr Jones was introduced as Clown in "The House That Jack Built's pantomime"; his expression and agility would make him the best clown on stage. Mr Lascelles was a great Harlequin."

Robinson Crusoe was the first pantomime loosely based upon a book.

In 1789. Later, other tales would become very popular. Dialog was becoming more important and new characters like the Fairy Queen were introduced.

The role of Principal Boy was established in the 1860s. In 1852, Miss Ellington was the first to be appointed Principal Boy. She was the 'Prince" in The Good Woman in the Wood at the Lyceum. Traditional pantomime critics were not impressed by the fact that the hero was a woman wearing tights.

Theatres felt pantomimes had to be modernized towards the end of 19th century. They were primarily intended for children, but theatres wanted to appeal to adults as well. So they introduced stars from music halls. They often brought their own style of comedy and songs.

Many innovations and changes occurred in the 20th century. To keep up, pantomimes had a need to change. Each theatre attempted to be the best by creating the largest spectacle possible and involving the most famous stars. Music halls were soon disregarded and radio stars were used to draw people to them. Television was born, and television stars were also employed. Today, pantomime is still up-to-date thanks to the use of modern technologies.

TUDOR & STUART

1511

1511

Katharine of Aragon was blessed with a son on New Years Day. His name was Henry. Henry VIII extended the Christmas court to celebrate. The baby survived for only seven weeks.

1532

Anne Boleyn was present at Henry VIII's Christmas court, although she didn't take part in the formal celebrations. Katherine of Aragon presided at the celebrations until she was succeeded by the King. Anne Boleyn was responsible for Christmas preparations starting around 1532

Elizabeth I

Robert Dudley, who is credited with giving the Queen the first wrist watch that was jewel-encrusted, received many extravagant gifts at Christmas.

The First Noel

Although it is not known where the poem originated, it is believed to have been written in 16th-century English. It was published for the first time in the William Sandys collection, which includes modern and ancient Christmas Carols.

Christ-kind (Christ Child)

The Protestant Reformation was a movement that took place both in Britain and Europe during the 16th- and 17th centuries. The Christ Child, a Protestant gift giver, discouraged St Nicholas. He is the gift-giver in the Czech Republic and Austria, Croatia, Luxembourg, Switzerland and parts of France. He is depicted as a figure of a cherub, wearing white clothes with small wings and blonde hair. Angels were not always male-only characters. They eventually became a part of nativity plays and included female angels.

The Christ kind can still be seen opening markets today. For decades, the Nuremberg Christ kind dressed in a long white gown and adorned with a golden crown has been a symbol for Christmas markets. The Christ kind's tasks don't stop there. She has a busy schedule until Christmas Eve, making appearances at children's markets, charity events, and hospitals across Europe as well as America.

Tradition has it that Christ-kind will not give children gifts if they try to see him.

Ding Dong Merrily on High

Unknown composer, but believed to be 16th-century. Original text in Latin: Gloria in Excelsis Deo

Tinsel

Although the origins of this decoration are not clear, it is believed to have originated in Germany around 1610. It was named das lametta after the Italian word 'lama' which means blade. These sheets of silver alloy were hammered to a very thin thickness. The sheets were then cut into strips. Although the lametta can be reused, it will lose its shine over time.

Legend of the Tinsel is about an elderly widow who spent Christmas Eve decorating a tree to give her children. After she was done, she went to bed. As she fell asleep, spiders climbed into the tree and spun their webs among the branches. The Christ Child saw all the webs and the tree, and knew that the widow would be disappointed. He touched the webs and made the room shine with a sparkling silver.

Tinsel arrived in Britain probably around 1846. In the Illustrated London News, Queen Victoria and Prince Albert are shown with a decorated tree that may have contained lametta.

Tinsel at this time was made from silver and was therefore only available to the very wealthy. A cheaper, more affordable version of tinsel was not available until the 1920s. In the 1930s, icicle tinsel was very popular. However, in 1950s aluminized papers were used. The downside was that it was dangerous for fire.

Today, tinsel is made of Polyvinyl Chloride and coated with a variety of metallic colours. It is now readily available for everyone.

Deck the Halls

It is believed that the music was Welsh-inspired and derived from the 16th-century winter carol Nos Galan. Thomas Oliphant, the lyricist, is credited with translating the Welsh into English and including it in "Welsh Melodies with Welsh and English Poetry", 1862.

Baubles

Lauscha, a small German mountain village, was known for its glassworks in 1597. Hans Greiner and Christopher Muller owned the glassworks, which made drinking glasses, bowls, and beads. It is located in

Although the origin of the glass ornament is not known, the earliest pieces were connected to form a chain.

After Queen Victoria's illustration, Baubles were popularized in Britain in 1846. Greiner was producing shapes, not just baubles, at this point. These were then exported to Europe with a silvery appearance due to their interior being coated with lead and mercury. The baubles were first exported to America in 1880s after F W Woolworth discovered them.

Germany was the dominant market for baubles for a long time. It eventually expanded into glass figures and toys. Japan and other countries began producing ornaments on an industrial scale in 1925, but this didn't affect the popularity of German-made ornaments.

Christmas Cake

This was originally a Plum Porridge that was eaten on Christmas Eve in late 16th-century England. Later, honey, dried fruit, spices and other ingredients were added. Because only the wealthy had ovens, it was boiled. In the 16th century, oatmeal was replaced by butter, wheat flour, and eggs to make a boiled plum cake. It was decorated with marzipan or almond sugar paste by those who could afford it.

To begin with, the cake was eaten at Easter. The addition of seasonal spices, representing the spices brought to the wise men, saw the cakes being introduced into the festive season. However, it was not eaten on Christmas Day but Twelfth Night.

Around the 1830s, a shift started towards Christmas Cake on Christmas Day. This was aided by Victorian bakers who decorated their cakes with snow scenes.
Christmas Cake is associated with Stir Up Sunday, the Sunday before Advent, and the unluckiness of cutting Christmas Cake before dawn on Christmas Eve.

Krampus

The Krampus, a bizarre figure, was first associated with Christmas in the 17th century.

It is a Germanic folklore-based beast, which has cloven hooves, horns like goats, long pointed tongue, and chains.

Oder bundles of birch branch branches.

The Krampus was portrayed as the antithesis of St Nicholas. He punished children for being naughty. The Krampusnacht was a celebration of St Nicholas Day. Young men dressed up as the Krampus, and walked the streets in rusty chains to scare children.

Through the 1800s, the Krampus was still popular and began appearing on greeting cards. A 1900s example shows a young girl carrying a basket of fruits and her brother beside her. The Krampus is wrapping her in a wicker basket.

On cards, the Krampus can also be seen as half man, half goat, or as a man wearing a dark suit and horns.

Sugar Plums

Sugar plum was a sweet made from sugar and a central kernel (an almond, for example) since the 17th century. You could also make them with caraway or cardamom seeds. The kernel was placed in a pan and allowed to cool while layers of sugar were added one after another.

The sweet was originally called a sugar plum, but the central piece of dried fruits could be any type. It was something that only the wealthy could afford before the advent of machinery. The sweet was costly and took many days to make.

Sugar had dropped in price by the 1860s and machines made it easier to make them. They were easily mass-produced and made available to everyone. They were hung on Christmas trees by many people.

Candy Canes

Although candy canes were not mentioned until the 19th Century, there is evidence that they existed in 17th-century America.

A Cologne Cathedral choir master had candy sticks made in the shape of a shepherd's crook and bent them into sticks. The practice was then spread to other children.

This story suggests that the candy canes may have been plain white, with later coloured stripes.

The Shepherds Observed Their Herds at Night

Nahum Tate, poet laureate of Queen Anne in 1703, wrote this poem. Nicholas Brady was also a co-author.

WHEN CHRISTMAS WAS BANNED

   Phillip Stubbes was an English Puritan and pamphleteer in the 1500s. He wrote "The Anatomie of Abuses In England" and commented on Christmas among other subjects.

"More mischief than ever is committed in the following year" - this includes what masking, mumming, and murder. Beyond the great dishonour to God and the impoverishment of the realm, this year's dicing, carding, eating, drinking, feasting, and banqueting is more common than ever before.

In the Stuart era, the 25th of December was a public holiday. All work places were closed. Church services were held. Presents were exchanged. There was also drinking, singing and stage performances. For the next 11 days, masses were held and the work day was cut shorter. The festivities culminated with a feast on Twelfth Night.

By the middle of the 1500s, England was no longer Catholic and was a Protestant nation. Christmas was a Catholic holiday and Protestant leaders started to discredit Catholic feast days and saints days. John Calvin and John Knox prefer to celebrate only where the Bible specifically says so. These Protestant leaders believed that Christmas was an epoch of the Catholic Church, and was not desired anymore. The Bible did not mention 25th December as a holiday and it also didn't mention drinking or eating too much. They concluded that Sunday, Easter, Christmas and all Saints Day should be observed with greater strictness.

With his Puritan forces, Oliver Cromwell was elected to power in 1644. He took steps to curtail Christmas' excesses. England tried to ban Christmas carol singing and snowballing in Scotland in 1583. It was believed that the celebration of Christmas was incompatible with core Christian beliefs. Anything associated with Christmas celebrations was illegal, even going to church.

There is no evidence Oliver Cromwell actually enforced this.A new Directory of Public Worship was created by parliament with help from church ministers to reorganise worship. It would be the only form of worship allowed in England and Wales. Only if there was biblical justification could be a festival be held and since, up until the reign of Henry VIII England had been a Catholic country, to end all feast days and saints days meant there probably wasn't much left.
In 1649 Cromwell had King Charles I executed and for the next four years England was ruled by Parliament. Then on 20 April 1653 Oliver Cromwell

expelled Parliament and made himself Lord Protector.

Cromwell was a Puritan and Puritans frowned upon pointless enjoyment. They lived their lives according to the Bible and believed a person must work hard in order to get into Heaven. As a result of beliefs Cromwell ordered all playhouses to be shut, sport was banned, inns were closed and people found working on the Sabbath were put into the stocks. No swearing was allowed, colourful clothes were banned. Women wore long black dresses with white aprons and head dresses. There was no make up. Men also had to dress in black and have short hair.

By now Christmas was an ordinary working day, shops and markets were open and people were fined if they went to church. Soldiers even patrolled the streets in London seizing any food deemed to be for Christmas.

In 1656 legislation was passed that made Sunday a day of rest and also the Catholic element of Christmas, 'Mass', was replaced with 'tide'.

The banning of Christmas was incredibly unpopular with people who felt the government had no right to be interfering with their beliefs. Riots took place and lives were lost in places such as London and Norwich between those who supported Christmas and those who didn't.

In 1660 the monarchy was restored and all legislation banning Christmas was dropped and people were free to celebrate Christmas again.

However even though people had secretly celebrated Christmas as best they could, or caused a public disturbance by rioting, people did eventually stop celebrating it altogether for fear of being fined. For around fifteen years Christmas was not celebrated. As a result traditions began to die out. There were no more Lords of Misrule, no singing in the streets, no feasting, houses could not be publicly decorated. The inns and theatres were closed so the mummers and carol singers had nowhere to call. No gifts were exchanged, no nativities. Just another day. Christmas really wouldn't be celebrated again properly again until Victorian times.

Poor Robin Almanac

By the 1700s Christmas was being observed once again but ways of celebrating had changed. In the period of time when it was banned, people had forgotten about the customs or died and not passed them on to the younger generation. Some people though did record the history of Christmas, William Wynstanley for example who somehow managed to keep his writing safe through the Puritan ban. He wrote that Christmas was a time when families and friends gathered together, homes were decorated with evergreens and log fires burned. It was a time of charity and open houses, a time of feasting and drinking. It was a time to play games, he mentions 'Hunt the Slipper', 'Shoe the Wild Mare' and 'Blind Man's Buff'. There were dances, carol singing, storytelling and feasting on beef, turkey, goose, duck, mince pies and plum pudding.

Around 1677 he wrote a poem that was published in the Monmouthshire Merlin newspaper on 26 December 1829.

Now grocers trade is in request
For plums and spices of the best
Good cheer doth with this month agree
And dainty chaps must sweetened be
Mirth and gladness doth abound
And strong beer in each house is found
Minced pies, roast beef with other cheer
And feasting doth conclude the year.

GEORGIAN
Boxing Day

Celebrated on the 26th December it was a day to open the alms boxes placed in churches on Christmas Day for worshippers to donate to the poor.

The day itself possibly originated in the late 18th century when the Lords of the manor boxed up their leftovers or gifts to give out to their tenants. The aristocracy also gave out presents (boxes) to their employees and servants who then had a day off to visit family and friends.

In 1871 Boxing Day became a national holiday in Britain and is now a time for sports, races and sales.

Charity

Charity played a great part at Christmas as it still does today. These acts were often recorded in newspapers such as in this article from the North Wales Gazette in 1812.

"On Christmas Day Mr Price, distributed by the hands of his worthy steward Mr Robert Hughes 1148 pounds of prime beef to about 300 families with 300 loaves of bread and upward of 601 worth of linsey and flannel to those who were in need; but the benevolence of this highly respected gentleman did not stop here, he gave at the same time a sum of money to every person to purchase plenty of strong ale to wash down the Roast Beef of Old England. We hope the very worthy donor will meet his reward both here and hereafter".

They also recorded what the rich were feasting on, this article is from the Cambrian newspaper of January 1808.

"At the last dinner given buy Earl Grosvenor to the Corporation of Chester, the most conspicuous dishes were, a baron of beef and a large Christmas pye which weighed 154 pounds. It contained three geese, three turkeys, seven hares, twelve partridges, a ham and a leg of veal"

The Decline of Christmas

In Colonial America in the year 1749. Peter Kalm, a Finnish-Swedish Naturalist was visiting Philadelphia and recorded his observations that

"One did not seem to know what it meant to wish anyone a merry Christmas – first the Presbyterians did not care much for celebrating Christmas but when they saw most of their members going to the English (Anglican) church on that day they also started to have services"
He also observed the Quakers.

"The Quakers did not regard this day (Christmas Day) any more remarkable than other days. Stores were open and anyone might sell or purchase what he wanted, There was no more baking of bread for the Christmas festival than for other days and no Christmas porridge on Christmas Eve!"

By 1827 Christmas was dying in Britain. Newspaper articles were recalling it with a mixture of nostalgia and disgust. This was printed in the North Wales Gazette on 16 February 1809.

"There was formerly a ridiculous festival celebrated at Christmas in France called the Feast of Fools, which continued til towards the latter end of the sixteenth century and was a mixture of religion and disgusting impiety. They used to elect a bishop and in some churches a pope of fools; the priests were debauched with dregs of wine and other filth and were masked and disguised in the most ridiculous manner. On entering the choir of Sens they began the office, which was composed by the Archbishop of that seat in the year 1222, when they danced and sung obscene songs; the deacons and sub deacons eat puddings at the altar before the celebrant and even played with cards and dice in his presence while they threw into the censor pieces of old shoe leather with which they perfumed him; they then dragged the deacons through the streets and threw them into carts or barrows full of ordure, at the same time putting themselves in lascivious postures and making indecent gestures"

Eighteen years later, this was printed in the Cambrian newspaper on 29 December.

"So early as 1599 Puritanism began to object to those sports of our ancestors and though in the provinces many local peculiarities are still kept up, most of the old customs (feasting excepted) continue to decline from year to year and will probably, at no distant period be totally extinct"

The Monmouthshire Merlin of 19 December 1829 printed an article in a similar vein.

"Shall we pass without comment the approach of Christmas? Pshaw! cries the lover of antiquated customs. We have no longer a Christmas. It is now but a name, the recollection of a delightful dream, the memory of a joyous pageant whose gaiety and excitement are no more"

So what were people doing during the Christmas period, this small article from the Carmarthen Journal printed on 18 December 1829 gives a small glimpse in what was happening in a town near there.

"A correspondent from Pembroke writes to inform us that the Christmas festivities of that town are likely to prove more than usually gay this season. The last week of the year is named as a hunt meeting, for their commencement when all the beauty and fashion of the town and neighbourhood have declared their intention to assemble and many of the best lodgings are already taken"

Joy To The World

Written in 1719 by Isaac Waters and based on psalm 98. The music was by George Frederick Handel.

Christmas Tree

The custom of the Christmas Tree began in Germany. Legend says that English Bishop Winifred (St Boniface, 675 - 754) went to Germany to preach about Christianity as a missionary. After a period of success he went to Rome to see Pope Gregory but upon his return to Germany found the people had reverted to their old practices of celebrating the Winter Solstice under Odin's Oak tree. Boniface was angry and took an axe and cut down the Oak. The people then asked how they should worship and Boniface pointed to a fir tree, symbolizing peace and immortality.

The Christmas tree may have been introduced to Britain as early as Georgian times. Queen Charlotte, wife of George III is said to have had a tree in the 1790s.

In the 1830s Queen Victoria is said to have recalled trees with lights and sugar ornaments. Queen Victoria loved Christmas as did Prince Albert and when the illustration of their tree appeared, in 1848, the popularity of the Christmas tree began to spread. By the 1880s the Norway Spruce became available and replaced the tree of choice at the time, the German Springelbaum.

Hark The Herald Angels Sing

Written by Charles Wesley in 1739, his brother was John Wesley the founder of the Methodist Church. In 1840 William H Cummings adapted music by Felix Mendelssohn to fit it, it originally had a different tune.

Poinsettia

In Central America the Poinsettia is called 'Flame Leaf'. It is a plant that flowers in the winter. The Aztecs called it Cuetlaxachitl and they used its flowers to make dye and to treat fevers.

There is a legend surrounding the Poinsettia that comes from Mexico and concerns a girl named Maria and her brother Pablo. Every year Maria and Pablo looked forward to Christmas when the village church would celebrate by displaying a manger, holding parties and parades. However Maria and Pablo were poor and it upset them that they were unable to buy presents and also give something to the baby Jesus.

One Christmas Eve they set out for the church service and on their way spotted some weeds growing at the side of the road. They decided to give these to the baby Jesus, even though the other children laughed at them. They were happy with what they had given though for they knew that they had given everything they could. As they lay the weeds around the manger, the top leaves turned bright red, just like the Star of Bethlehem.

The Poinsettia became popular in other parts of the world when, in 1825, the first U S Ambassador to Mexico, Joel Roberts began growing them and giving them to friends.

Adeste Fideles (O Come All Ye Faithful)

First published in 1751 and generally attributed to John Francis Wade.

The Twelve Days of Christmas

First published in England in 1780. The tune associated with it today is from 1909 and was composed by Frederic Austin.

Christmas Robin

The Robin adorns many Christmas cards, usually in a snowy scene or sat on a post box. It is thought it was named after postmen in 1784 who were called 'Redbreasts' because their uniforms were scarlet with blue lapels and red waistcoats. It is possible too that the Christmas Robin could have been named after the Poor Robin Almanac as a tribute to the wiring of William Wynstanley and his recording of Christmas traditions during the Puritan ban. There is also a legend of the Robin connecting it to the Christmas Nativity.

In the cold stable, just after Jesus was born, the fire was beginning to die. Mary asked all the animals if they could keep it alight but none came forward to do so. Then, a little Robin flew down and began fanning the flames with his wings. Every now and then he flew away, returning with twigs to put on the fire. As he continued to fan the flames, sparks turned his chest red. Mary was grateful for the warmth of the fire and declared the Robin's chest would always be red as a symbol of having a good heart.

The Baddeley Cake

In 1795 the Drury Lane Theatre, London provided a Twelfth Night cake for its performers. In the will of actor Robert Baddeley he requested that each year on the 6th January cake and punch was to be provided for the company in residence.

To begin with the manager of the theatre was responsible but later the Drury Lane Theatrical Fund have organised the event. By 1890 the cake was being cut on stage with guests numbering around two thousand but by 1892 the cake was cut in a dressing room with just the company present.

In modern times the cake has taken on the theme of the current musical and in the tradition of Twelfth Night cakes are amazingly elaborate. The theme for the 2014 cake was Charlie and the Chocolate Factory.

Washington Irving

Best known for writing the Legend of Sleepy Hollow and Rip Van Winkle, however he also wrote about Christmas and is one of the authors who contributed to how we celebrate Christmas today.

In 1812, using the pseudonym Diedrich Knickerbocker he wrote in the History of New York of St Nicholas in a dream sequence

"riding over the tops of trees in that self same wagon wherein he brings his yearly presents to children"

He also wrote 'The Sketch Book'; a collection of five Christmas stories based on the old fashioned customs at an English manor. The inspiration had come from his time staying at Aston hall, Birmingham. His pseudonym for this was Geoffrey Crayon and the English manor, Bracebridge Hall.

"The Squire went on to lament the deplorable decay of the games and amusements which were once prevalent at this season among the lower orders and countenanced by the higher, when the old halls of castles and manor houses were thrown open at daylight; when tables were covered with brawn and beef and humming ale; when the harp and the carol resounded all day long and when rich and poor were alike welcome to enter and make merry. Our old games and local customs said he, had a great effect in making the peasant fond of his home and the promotion of them by the gentry made him fond of his lord. They made the times merrier, kinder and better"

Silent Night

The lyrics were written in 1816 by priest Joseph Mohr. The music was composed in 1818 by Franz Xavier Gruber a school master and was first performed in 1818 at St Nicholas parish church, Obendorf, Austria.

Reindeer

The first written account of reindeer in association with Christmas is probably that of a poem included in a booklet published by William Gilley in New York in 1821. The booklet was called 'A New Year's Present' and the author of the poem was anonymous but in it reindeer are introduced.
"Old Sante Claus with much delightful
His reindeer drives this frosty night O'er
chimney tops and tracks of snow To
bring his yearly gifts to you"

According to Gilley the author had been told of reindeer that lived near the Arctic by his mother, an Indian and that they could fly.

Rudolph the Red Nosed Reindeer first appeared in a book by Robert L May and published by Montgomery Ward. It was adapted into a song and recorded by Gene Autry on 27 June 1949.

A Visit from St Nicholas

Also known as 'The Night Before Christmas', this poem was published by Troy Sentinel in 1823. It was written by Clement Clarke Moore for his children. Moore was an American professor of Oriental and Greek literature and wrote the poem during a visit to his cousin, Mary McVicker.

The poem solved the mystery of how St Nicholas comes down the chimney, by using a miniature sleigh. It redefined the image of Christmas, of Santa's appearance and also included the names of the reindeer, though Rudolph was not included at this time he was a much later addition.

It is believed a family friend sent 'A Visit From St Nicholas' to the New York Sentinel. The condition of publication was that the author had to remain anonymous but in 1844 Moore claimed ownership when it was included in a book of his poems.

Today 'A Visit From St Nicholas' is read all over the world and in may places has become traditional to read it on Christmas Eve.

VICTORIAN

A Christmas Carol

One of Washington Irving's fans was Charles Dickens. At a dinner hosted by Irving, Dickens said

"I say gentlemen, I do not go to bed two nights out of seven without taking Washington Irving with me"

By the time Charles Dickens wrote A Christmas Carol, the Industrial Revolution was well under way and Christmas for most was just another working day. Christmas must have felt very dull to Dickens or anyone else reading Irving's descriptions of Christmases past at Bracebridge Hall.

Although this may have inspired Dickens, he didn't write of Irving's quaint country manor Christmases. He wrote of what he knew, Christmas for the middle and lower classes, the suffering of children due to the Industrial Revolution and swapped snowy landscapes for harsh fog filled London.

Today, its most famous character is Scrooge, known for being miserly and having no interest in Christmas. However, to understand the Scrooge character we have to remember it was written in 1843, in Britain Christmas pretty much existed in name only as we have already seen from newspaper articles of the time. How was Scrooge to keep Christmas in the atmosphere of apathy towards it.

So Scrooge is visited by four ghosts, Jacob Marley who tells him it's not too late to change. The Ghost of Christmas Past, who takes him to Fezziwig's warehouse, transformed into a ballroom for his employees, to remind him of Christmases past when all were made to feel equal and valued. The Ghost of Christmas Present tells Scrooge it's not too late to get to know him. Christmas still exists, all he has to do is make the effort. He is also shown Tiny Tim, his employee Bob Cratchit's child who is ill. Then the Ghost of Christmas Future shows Scrooge he is mortal and if he doesn't change his thoughts and actions Christmas will die, as well as Tiny Tim. Scrooge has the power to change, and he does so, waking Christmas morning and providing a turkey and a pay rise for Bob Cratchit, looking after his poor employee, just like the employers of old and ensuring that Christmas was kept.

A Christmas Carol was written in the Autumn of 1843 and published on December 19th of the same year. All six thousand copies sold out straight away and the book has never gone out of print.

Christmas Cards

Sir Henry Cole, an entrepreneur invented the Christmas Card in 1843 as a way of saving time. Instead of spending hours letter writing at Christmas, a card could convey his thoughts, wishes and greetings for him. He had a friend, an artist by the name of John Horsley who set about designing and creating. A thousand lithographs were produced at first but the cards became so popular and combined with affordable postal rates caught on very quickly. Christmas scenes were popular, as were robins, evergreens and Father Christmas though he wasn't always dressed in red.

In 2001, one of Coles cards, which he had written to his grandmother sold at auction for £22,500.

Christmas Lights

In 1848 the Illustrated London News showed Queen Victoria and her family celebrating around a lit Christmas tree. Electric lights were well into the future so the Queen's tree was lit with candles. These candles were pinned or glued on to the branches.

In 1880 Joseph Swan patented the light bulb in Britain and started producing strings of lights around 1882. Of course only the rich could afford to buy them.

Candle holders began to be used from around 1890. However if the candle was too heavy it caused the branches to droop, tipping hot wax everywhere or worse setting fire to the house.

In the early 20th century, lanterns to hold candles was a much safer option. In 1935 Selfridges began selling illuminated trees but it wasn't really until after the Second World War and into the 1950's that lights became used more widely. Businesses, in London for example, began clubbing together to buy lights for the streets (Regents Street Association and Oxford Street etc) though there were times when lack of funds meant no lights.

Christmas Crackers

Tom Smith was an apprentice confectioner in London in the early 19th century. In 1846 he went off on a trip top Paris and while he was there saw some bon bons wrapped in brightly coloured tissue paper. Inspired, he returned to London and decided to create something similar himself. However he wanted to create something different, more exciting and new. So, into his coloured wrappers he inserted a strip of paper coated in chemicals, which, when rubbed together created a popping sound. Also he eventually included a motto and poem.

After he died his two sons continued with his cracker business, adding the paper crown in the 1900s and by the 1930s the poems had been replaced by jokes.

Artificial Tree

The artificial tree originated in Germany about 1845. To begin with they were quite small, designed to stand on a table. They were made from wire covered in feathers and attached to a larger wire. The feathers could be goose, swan or ostrich and coloured green.

After the death of Queen Victoria, Christmas trees experienced a decline in popularity, unlike real trees which by the 1930's were a booming industry. During the Second World War though artificial ones started to make a comeback as they could be easily moved into an air raid shelter.

After the war Germany carried on making feather trees and started producing them in different colours.

The first brush tree was manufactured by an American company called

Addis Brush Co. who made toilet brushes, around 1930. The brush trees were much stronger than the feather ones and could hold more weight in decorations. Their silver pine tree of the 1950s was aluminium and also had a revolving light in the bottom.

O Holy Night

Composed by Adolphe Adam in 1847 the words were from a poem, Midnight Christians by Placide Cappeau.

It Came Upon a Midnight Clear
This began as a poem written by Edmund Hamilton Sears in 1849. Music was added by Richard Storrs Willis in 1859.

Once in Royal David's City

Written by Mrs C F Alexander (1818 – 1895). She was the wife of the Bishop of Derry and write mainly for children.

We Three Kings

Written by Reverend John Henry Hopkins in 1857 for a General Theological Seminary Christmas Pageant in New York City.

Jingle Bells

Written buy James Lord Pierpont and published in 1857 with the title One Horse Open Sleigh. It was written for Thanksgiving and inspired by sleigh races.
Angels We Have Heard on high

Based on a French Carol, 'Angels in our Countryside', the author is unknown but the English version was translated by James Chadwick in 1862.

What Child Is This

In 1865, while seriously ill, bedridden and depressed, William Chadderton Dix wrote this song to the tune of Greensleeves.

Christmas Annuals

The Christmas Annual may have its origins in the bound volumes of weekly or monthly magazine issues that appeared in the early 1800s..

One of the first regular annuals was Beetons Christmas Annual that ran from 1860 to 1898. It was published by Samuel Orchart Beeton and in 1887 featured a novel by Arthur Conan Doyle called 'A Study in Scarlet' which included the debut of characters Sherlock Holmes and Dr Watson.

In the 1900s the content began to change. Publishers began to pint new material and aim the books at children e.g, Blackies Children's Annual. After World War One regular titles began to appear such as Rover, Wizard, Rainbow and Tiger Tim. Then in the 1920s when comic strips appeared in newspapers, they too had their own annual, e.g, teddy Tail from the Daily Mail and Rupert the Bear from the Daily Express.

The birth of cinema, radio and television meant that today a huge range of titles are available.

O Little Town Of Bethlehem

Rector Phillip Brooks wrote the lyrics in 1862 after being inspired by the hills of Palestine and Bethlehem. Music was by Lewis Redner.

Santa's Grotto

A British tradition that began in 1879 and spread to other parts of the world. The grotto is a cavern filled with lights, music and characters such as elves and reindeer. There is also Santa of course who gives out a gift to children who visit.

The first grotto was in Lewis's Bon Marche Department Store in Liverpool 1879 and it was named Christmas Fairyland.

In 1896 John Martin's Department Store had a magic cave and by 1933 a whole pageant came into being where Santa would arrive and be escorted to the grotto when Christmas could them officially begin.

The grottoes are still a prominent part of Christmas today and can include animated reindeer and elves. They have evolved in some stores to take up an entire floor, such as Santa Land at Macy's New York or Selfridges where children have been able to ride the Santa express and be greeted by elves at a station before meeting Santa.

Santa's Workshop

In 1879 Thomas Nast was a cartoonist for Harper's Weekly. He created a series of drawings showing Santa's workshop at the North Pole.

In Finnish folklore though the place of Santa's Workshop is at Korvatunturi in Lapland among lakes, pine trees and reindeer. It is situated in an ear shaped fell which allows Santa to hear all the wishes of children.

Holly Beating

This is a custom unique to Wales but died out by the end of the 19th century. Young men and boys would gather holly branches and beat the unprotected arms of young women until they bled. In some areas it was the legs that were beaten and in others it was the last person in bed who was subjected to the holly branch.

Away in a Manger

Published in 1885 the music was by William J Kirkpatrick but the author of the lyrics is unknown

Mrs Claus

Santa's wife first gets a mention in a short story from 1849 written by James Rees of Philadelphia. The story tells the tale of an old man and woman who are given shelter for the night on Christmas Eve. In the morning the children of their host find toys and gifts from the couple who in the end turn out to be the host's long lost daughter and husband and not 'old Santa Claus and his wife'.

Mrs Claus is often shown as a white haired, kind elderly woman as in the illustrations for Katharine Lee Bates' poem 'Goody Santa Claus on a Sleigh Ride' from 1889.

In 1919 a postcard shows Mrs Claus in similar clothing to her husband saying goodbye as he sets off on his journey and her role hasn't really changed that much except today she is known for caring for the reindeer, preparing the toys and making cookies with the elves.